PUZZLE TIME!

MY AWESOME PUZZLE BOOK

D1514933

ARCTURUS

ARCTURUS

This edition published in 2011 by Arcturus Publishing Limited
26/27 Bickels Yard, 151–153 Bermondsey Street,
London SE1 3HA

ISBN: 978-1-84837-503-1
CH001403EN

Created by Small World Design
Additional design by Omnipress

Printed in Singapore

Jigsaw Puzzle

Which piece fits exactly into the puzzle?

Fruit Anagrams

Unscramble the words to find the names of different types of fruit.
We've given you the first letter of each word to help you!

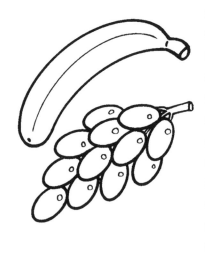

pleap   a _ _ _ _ _

rerych   c _ _ _ _ _ _

perag   g _ _ _ _ _

lump   p _ _ _

brawrstrey s _ _ _ _ _ _ _ _ _

tropica   a _ _ _ _ _ _ _

cheap   p _ _ _ _

melon   l _ _ _ _ _

Memory Test

Look carefully at the picture of the boy's desk for one minute, then turn the page to answer some questions!

Memory Test

How many things can you remember from the picture on the previous page?
No peeking!

1. How many sheets of paper are there?

2. Are all the pencils the same length?

3. What is on top of the book?

4. Is the buckle on the bag open or closed?

5. What symbol is on the pencil case?

6. Is there a comb on the table?

7. What is between the tie and the ruler?

8. How many stripes are there on the tie?

Odd One Out

Look at the marching soldiers. Which is the odd one out?

Spot the Difference

Can you spot six differences between picture A and picture B?

Maze

Help the camel to walk through the desert to the oasis!

Colour the Picture

Four the Same

Can you find the four fish that are exactly the same?

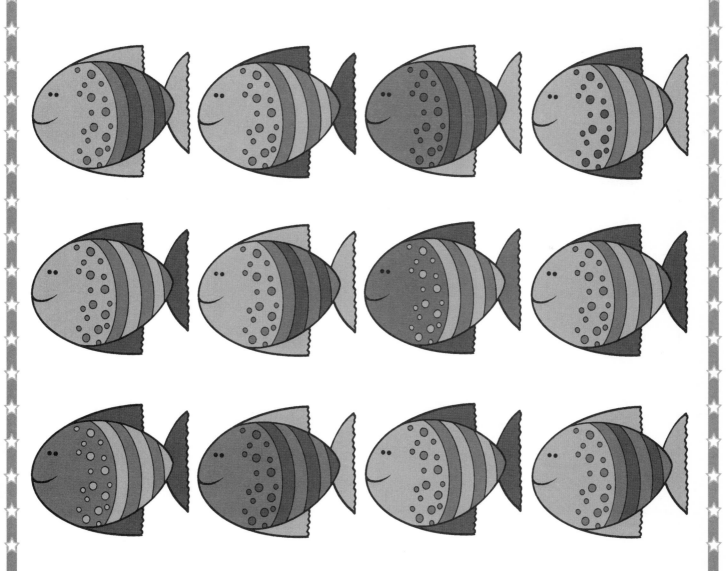

Crack the Code

Answer the questions to crack the code and solve the sum!

A   The number of tails on a dog

B   The number of horseshoes on a horse

C   The number of sides on a pentagon

D   The number of Snow White's dwarves

Hidden Picture

Shade the dotted shapes to find the hidden picture!

13

Jigsaw Puzzle

Which piece fits exactly into the puzzle?

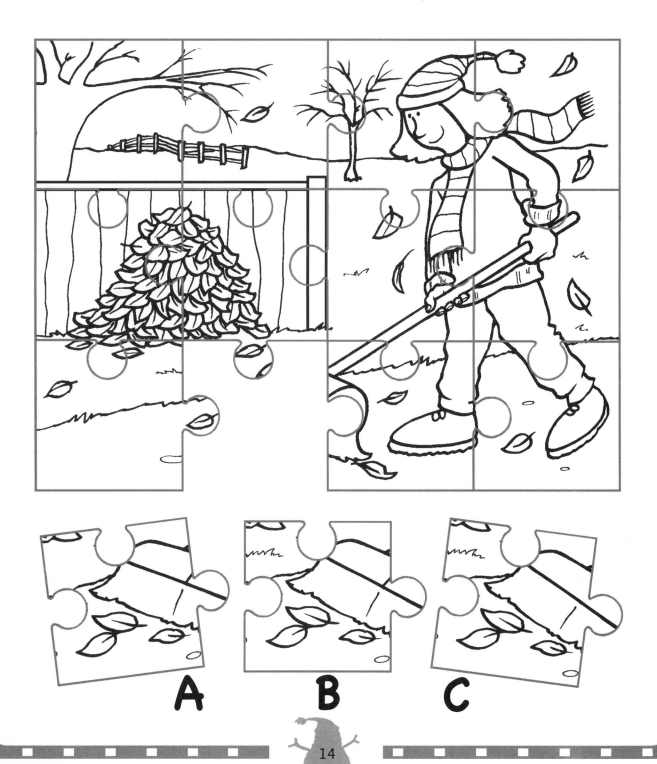

A **B** **C**

Follow the Trails

Which trail leads the detective to each object?

Snowman

Finish off the picture of the snowman using the grid to help you!

Memory Test

Look carefully at the picture of the birthday party for one minute, then turn the page to answer some questions!

Memory Test

How many things can you remember from the picture on the previous page?
No peeking!

1. How many balloons are there?

2. What is the pattern on the girl's hat?

3. Are the candles on the cake lit?

4. What is in the open present?

5. How many long balloons are there?

6. What has the boy got on his T shirt?

7. Is the girl wearing a long- or short- sleeved top?

8. What sort of hat is the boy wearing?

Sport Anagrams

Unscramble the words to find the names of different sports.
We've given you the first letter of each word to help you!

flabloot   f _ _ _ _ _ _ _

nestin   t _ _ _ _ _

ginkis   s _ _ _ _ _

necfing   f _ _ _ _ _ _

chokey   h _ _ _ _ _

ectrick   c _ _ _ _ _ _

harecry   a _ _ _ _ _ _

ataker   k _ _ _ _ _

Odd One Out

Look at the electric guitars. Which is the odd one out?

Spot the Difference

Can you spot six differences between picture A and picture B?

Maze

Help the mouse to run through the trap to the cheese!

Colour the Picture

Two the Same

Can you find the two pairs of socks that are exactly the same?

Crack the Code

Answer the questions to crack the code and let the spy into the laboratory!

A   The number of events in a decathlon

B   The number of senses you have

C   The number of seconds in a minute

D   The number of sides on a cube

Hidden Picture

Shade the dotted shapes to find the hidden picture!

Jigsaw Puzzle

Which piece fits exactly into the puzzle?

A   **B**   **C**

Follow the Trails

Follow the trails to find out who has won each prize!

Vampire

Finish off the picture of the vampire using the grid to help you!

Space Anagrams

Unscramble the words to find different words about space.
We've given you the first letter of each word to help you!

crotek   r _ _ _ _ _

mecot   c _ _ _ _

netpal   p _ _ _ _ _

remote   m _ _ _ _ _

unotastar   a _ _ _ _ _ _ _ _

sleepcote   t _ _ _ _ _ _ _ _

latestile   s _ _ _ _ _ _ _ _

laxagy   g _ _ _ _ _

Memory Test

Look carefully at the picture of the girl's bedroom for one minute, then turn the page to answer some questions!

Memory Test

How many things can you remember from the picture on the previous page?
No peeking!

1. Which two objects are on the bedside cabinet?

2. How many drawers does the cabinet have?

3. What is on the cover of the girl's magazine?

4. Is she wearing a necklace?

5. What is the pattern on the window blind?

6. What can you see out of the window?

7. How many books are there on the top shelf?

8. What is sitting on the floor?

Odd One Out

Look at the speckled lizards. Which is the odd one out?

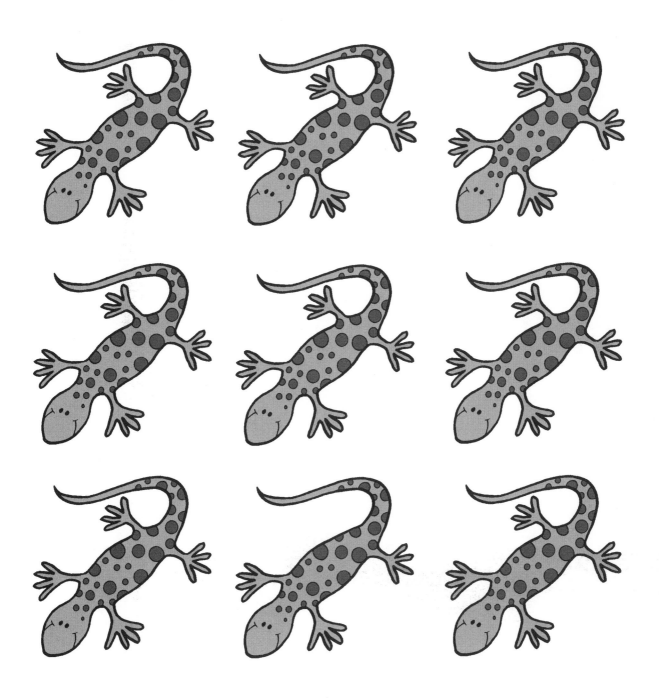

Spot the Difference

Can you spot six differences between picture A and picture B?

Maze

Help the bee to fly through the garden to reach the flower!

Colour the Picture

Three the Same

Can you find the three umbrellas that are exactly the same?

Crack the Code

Answer the questions to crack the code and help the cyclist to unlock his bicycle!

A   The number of ears on a hippo

B   The number of letters in the alphabet

C   The number of books in a trilogy

D   The number of years in half a century

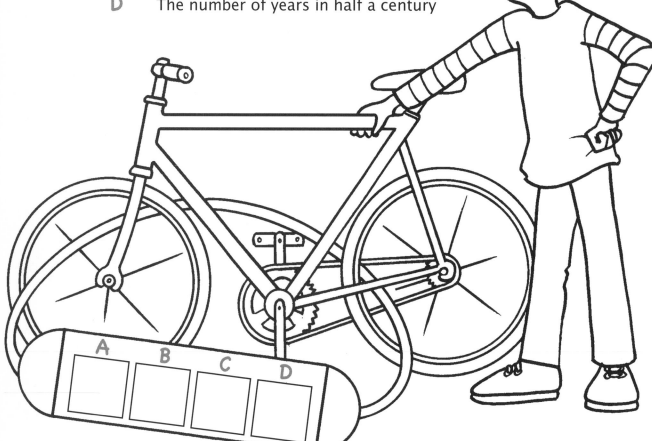

Hidden Picture

Shade the dotted shapes to find the hidden picture!

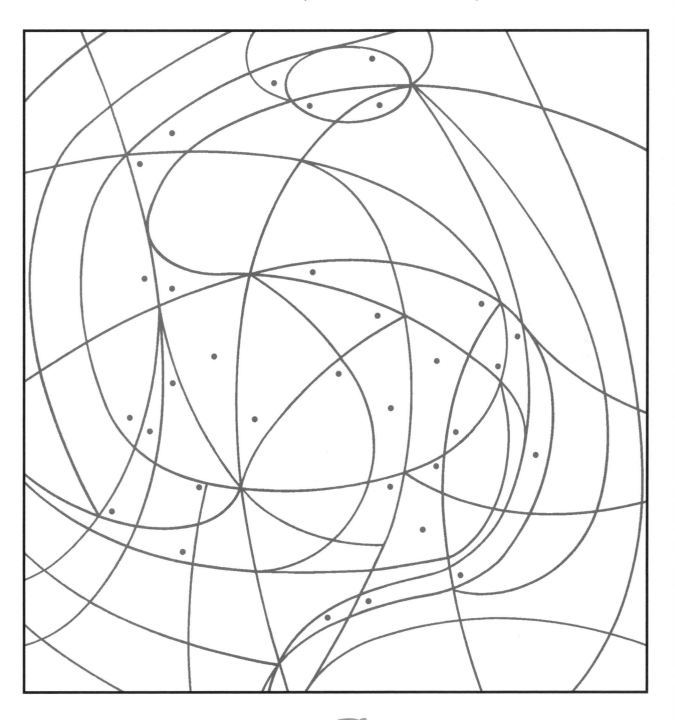

Jigsaw Puzzle

Which piece fits exactly into the puzzle?

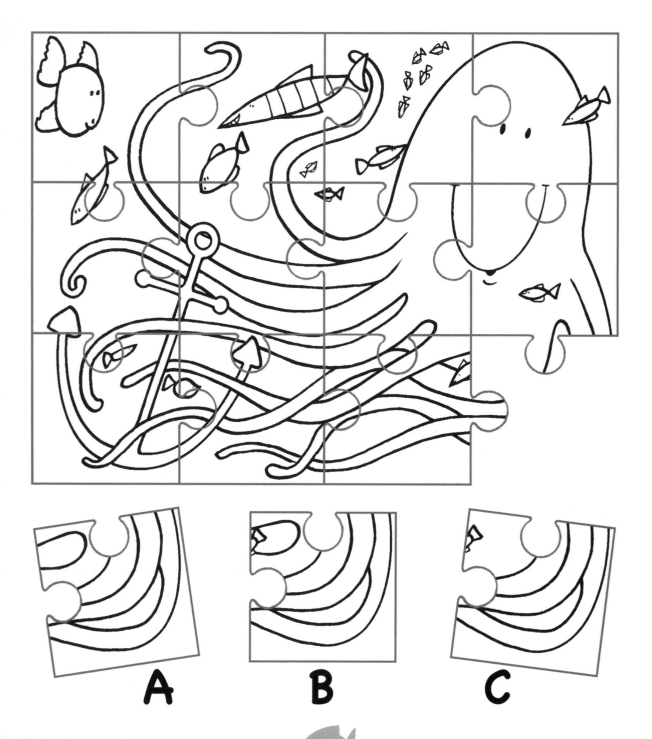

A   **B**   **C**

Follow the Trails

Follow the trails to see who is wearing which party hat!

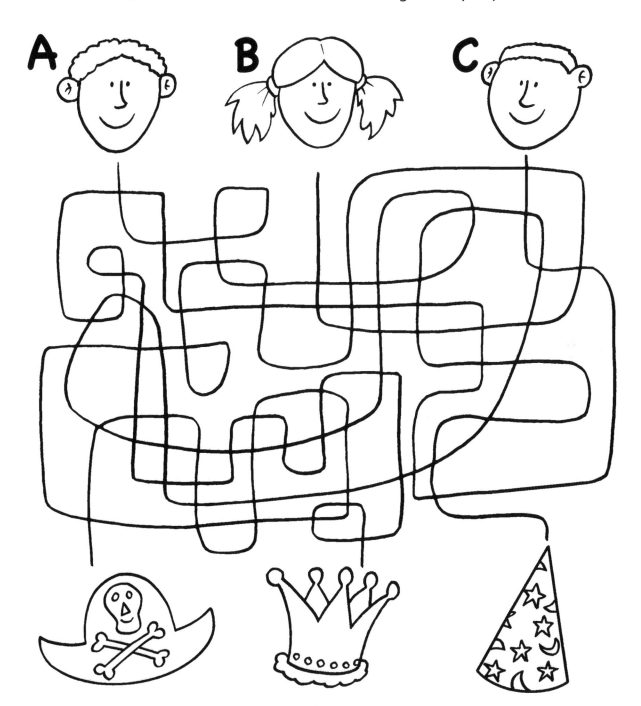

Juggler

Finish off the picture of the juggler using the grid to help you!

Memory Test

Look carefully at the picture of the seaside for one minute, then turn the page to answer some questions!

Memory Test

How many things can you remember from the picture on the previous page?
No peeking!

1. How many flags are there on the sandcastle?

2. Is the boy's hat on the right way?

3. What is the crab holding?

4. Are there any clouds in the sky?

5. Is the girl wearing shorts or a skirt?

6. What number is on the sail of the left-hand yacht?

7. Is the boy wearing sandals?

8. How many birds are there?

Answers

Page 3 – Jigsaw Puzzle
Piece A

Page 4 – Fruit Anagrams
Apple
Cherry
Grape
Plum
Strawberry
Apricot
Peach
Lemon

Page 6 – Memory Test
1. Three
2. No
3. A banana
4. Open
5. Star
6. Yes
7. Two sweets
8. Four

Page 7 – Odd One Out

Page 8 – Spot the Difference

Page 9 – Maze

Page 11 – Four the Same

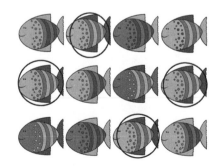

Page 12 – Crack the Code
14 + 57 = 71

Page 13 – Hidden Picture –
Eagle

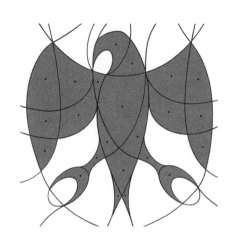

Page 14 – Jigsaw Puzzle
Piece B

Page 15 – Follow the Trails
Trail A leads to the camera.
Trail B leads to the disguise.
Trail C leads to the gloves.
Trail D leads to the
magnifying glass.

Page 18 – Memory Test
1. Five
2. Stripes
3. Yes
4. A torch
5. Two
6. A star
7. Long sleeved
8. A crown

Page 19 – Sport Anagrams

Football
Tennis
Skiing
Fencing
Hockey
Cricket
Archery
Karate

Page 20 – Odd One Out

Page 21 – Spot The Difference

Page 22 – Maze

Page 24 – Two the Same

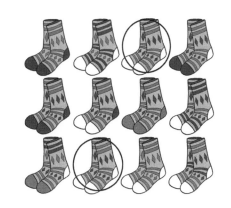

Page 25 – Crack the Code

A	B	C	D
10	5	60	6

Page 26 – Hidden Picture – Horse

Page 27 – Jigsaw Puzzle

Piece C

Page 28 – Follow the Trails

A has won a mobile phone.
B has won a watch.
C has won a radio.
D has won a camera.

Page 30 – Space Anagrams

Rocket
Comet
Planet
Meteor
Astronaut
Telescope
Satellite
Galaxy

Page 32 – Memory Test

1. A lamp and a clock
2. Three
3. A horse
4. Yes
5. Flowers
6. A tree
7. Five
8. A teddy bear

Page 33 – Odd One Out

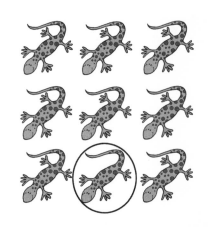

Page 34 – Spot the Difference

Page 35 – Maze

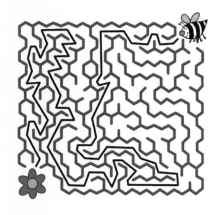

Page 37 – Three the Same

Page 38 – Crack the Code

A	B	C	D
2	26	3	50

Page 39 – Hidden Picture – Dinosaur

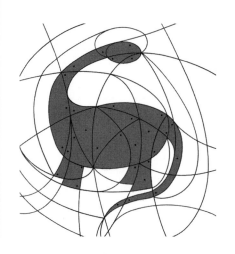

Page 40 – Jigsaw Puzzle Piece B

Page 41 – Follow the Trails

A is wearing the wizard's hat.
B is wearing the pirate's hat.
C is wearing the crown.

Page 44 – Memory Test

1. Two
2. Yes
3. A shell
4. Yes
5. A skirt
6. Seven
7. No
8. Three